THE LUNCH BOOK

KINNY KREISWIRTH & JOLENE BODILY, R.D. • ILLUSTRATED BY KINNY KREISWIRTH

Tambourine Books • New York

A SOMERVILLE HOUSE BOOK

Inquiries should be addressed to

Tambourine Books,
a division of William Morrow & Company, Inc.,
1350 Avenue of the Americas,
New York, New York
10019

Library of Congress Cataloging in Publication
Data

Kreiswirth, Kinny.
   The lunch book and bag: a fit kid's guide to
making delicious (and nutritious) lunches/
Kinny Kreiswirth & Jolene Bodily: illustrated
by Kinny Kreiswirth.—1st U.S. ed. p. cm.
   Summary: Information on packing a lunch
that is wise and nutritious.
   ISBN 0-688-11624-8
   1. Luncheons—Juvenile literature. 2.
Nutrition—Juvenile literature. 3. Lunchbox
cookery—Juvenile literature.
   [1. Lunchbox cookery. 2. Cookery. 3.
Nutrition] I. Bodily, Jolene. II. Title.
   TX735.K74 1992
   613.2—dc20   92-2815CIP AC

First Edition

A Somerville House Book
3080 Yonge Street, Suite 5000
Toronto, Ontario, M4N 3N1

Printed in Hong Kong
Bag manufactured and kit assembled in China.

Design by Kinny Kreiswirth and John Lee

Dedication:

To Aaron, Nathan, and Hannah, and
to Adam, Diana, Jill, and Rachel,
whose eating habits inspired this
book. And to Marty and Sam, whose
technical, physical, and moral support
helped make this book happen.

Thanks to: Beth Huff, B.P.H.E., B.Ed.,
physical education consultant. And to
friends, relatives, and nutritionists
who helped in many ways.

Table of Contents

Your Body Needs You

Has your stomach ever growled at you in the middle of the day?

It's lunch time, you're hungry, and you'll eat just about anything to satisfy that rumbling. But not everything you munch on satisfies your body.

The point is, your body needs proper maintenance and care for top performance. And that means good food, exercise, and sleep.

But how do you know what food is best for you? That's how the Lunch Book can help. It tells you all about food and what it does for you and your body. Before you know it, you will have worked out a terrific routine of healthy eating and exercise.

Begin filling in the Fit Stats Chart that comes with this package. Then use the Shop Fit List, charts, tips, recipes, and helpful information about food in this book. Get cooking and pack your culinary creations into your Lunch Bag. Enjoy every last bite!

You Are What You Eat ... and Do

Have you ever heard the expression, "You are what you eat?" Well, in a sense you are, because food helps your body grow and stay strong, healthy, and active. But you are also "what you do," because the exercise and rest you give your body work together with the food you eat to make you strong, healthy, and energetic.

Different foods contain different amounts of ingredients called nutrients: carbohydrates, vitamins, proteins, minerals, fiber, fats, and water. Each nutrient benefits your body in different ways. Foods are grouped by the different nutrients they contain. These are called food groups or families.

Take your first step towards developing a new fitness routine, by studying this chart.

This chart shows:

INPUT:
Each food group or activity, and the nutrients in each group.

OUTPUT:
The main benefit from each food group.

INPUT
FOOD GROUP
GRAINS
FRUITS & VEGETABL
PROTEINS
DAIRY
WATER
EXERCISE & SLEEP

OUTPUT

NUTRIENTS

BENEFITS

carbohydrates
vitamins
proteins
minerals
fiber

ENERGY

carbohydrates
vitamins
fiber

HEALTH

protein
minerals
fats

GROWTH

vitamins
protein
minerals
fats

STRENGTH

water

CIRCULATION

STRENGTH & PEP

Launching a Lunch

T he Shop Fit List on the opposite page is your key chart for choosing foods that will make a nutritious and balanced lunch. Foods with LOTS of nutritional value are found in the yellow area. Foods with LESS value are found in the white area, and foods with the LEAST value are found in the red area. Study the list carefully, start thinking about what you want for lunch, and figure out the nutritional value of each food you choose.

A helpful hint: a potato falls under the Fruits and Vegetables group and is found in the yellow area. That means it has LOTS of nutritional value and is among the best foods for your body. French fried potatoes are in the same food group, but are found in the white area. They have LESS nutritional value because frying adds fat and takes away nutrients. Finally, potato chips are found in the red area because even more fat has been added in preparing them. Therefore, they have the LEAST value of all.

The Shop Fit Pad

Hang your Shop Fit List pad that comes with this package in the kitchen. Whenever you think of a food that you'd like to eat, circle it. Try to keep your body's nutrient needs in mind using the LOTS, LESS, LEAST color guide. Encourage your whole family to use the list. And don't forget the list when you go shopping for food. One final tip: be sure to read pages 46-47 about how to read food labels at the supermarket.

The Shop Fit List

	GRAINS	FRUITS & VEGETABLES		PROTEINS	DAIRY	OTHER	

LOTS OF NUTRITIONAL VALUE	bagels
	biscuits
	bran
	bread
	bread sticks
	bulgur
	buns
	English muffins
	low-fat crackers
	pasta
	plain popcorn
	pretzels
	rice
	rice cakes
	rolls
	tortillas
	unsweetened &
	  cooked cereals
		applesauce
		  (unsweetened)
		apples
		apricots
		bananas
		blueberries
		cantaloupe
		cherries
		fruit canned in
		  water or juice
		grapefruit
		grapes
		kiwis
		mangoes
		nectarines
		oranges
		papayas
		peaches
		pears
		pineapple
		plums
		raspberries
		strawberries
		tangerines
		watermelon
		100% fruit juice
			asparagus
			beets
			broccoli
			brussels sprouts
			cabbage
			carrots
			cauliflower
			celery
			corn
			cucumbers
			eggplant
			green beans
			lettuce
			mushrooms
			onions
			peas
			peppers
			potatoes
			radishes
			spinach
			sprouts
			squash
			sweet potatoes
			tomatoes
			vegetable juice
			vegetable soup
			zucchini
				dried beans
				dried peas
				fish
				hummus
				lean beef
				lean lamb
				lean pork
				lentils
				light meat poultry
				  (no skin)
				refried beans
				tofu
				tuna in water
					non-fat/low-fat:
					  cottage cheese
					  milk
					  plain yogurt
					part-skim cheese:
					  feta
					  mozzarella
					  neufchatel
					  ricotta
					  string cheese
					pot cheese
						herbs & spices
						lemon juice
						mineral water
						mustard
						salsa
						seltzer water
						taco sauce
						vinegar
						water
							LOTS

				chicken hot dogs
				dark meat poultry
				  (with or without skin)
				eggs
				fried foods
				ham
				meat loaf
				nuts
				peanut butter
				peanuts
				red meat
				seeds
				tuna in oil
					cheese spread
					chocolate milk
					cream soups
					creamed cottage
					  cheese
					ice milk
					low-fat frozen yogurt
					regular cheese
					sweet yogurt
					whole milk
						bouillon
						consommé
						ketchup
						pickles
						pickle relish
							LESS

LESS	butter popcorn
	granola
	french toast
	high-fat crackers
	muffins
	pancakes/waffles
	sweetened cereals
						fats:
						  butter
						  gravy
						  margarine
						  mayonnaise
						  oil
						  salad dressing
						  tartar sauce
						sweets:
						  candy
						  chewing gum
						  chocolate
						  honey
						  jello
						  popsicles
						  soft drinks
						  sugar
						  syrup
							LEAST NUTRITIONAL VALUE

LEAST	cake & cookies cereals (sugar 1st) croissants doughnuts granola bars pies & pastries taco chips	dried fruit fruit in syrup fruit roll-ups raisins fruit drinks jam & jelly	avocados french fries olives potato chips	bacon bologna hot dogs pepperoni salami sausage	cream cheese cream sauces ice cream shakes sherbet sour cream whipped cream		

Let's Make Lunch

Remember to follow the kitchen code before you cook up a recipe:

1. Get an adult's permission and help, especially if you need to use the oven or stove, knives, or appliances.

2. Roll up your sleeves, put on an apron, and wash your hands.
3. Check all ingredients.
4. Be careful with knives, use a cutting board, and cut with the blade away from you.

5. Before plugging in an appliance, be sure it's turned off and your hands are dry.
6. Use pot holders and be sure to turn off the stove or oven when you're done cooking.
7. Clean up as you work and when you are done.
8. When you've finished your creation, get the pots, pans, dishes, and utensils right into some hot soapy water or rinsed and into the dishwasher. If they lie around getting dry and crusty, it takes a lot more hot water energy to get them clean.

Lunch in a Bag

The Lunch Bag that comes with this package makes it easy to carry your lunch to school, or on an outing or picnic. You can prepare your food ahead of time, pack it in your bag, and pop it in the refrigerator to keep it fresh. When you come home, empty the bag and shake out any crumbs. Keep it clean by washing it every now and then.

Try these lunch-bag tips to help you enjoy your lunch:

Food Tips
- Use fresh ingredients or freshly cooked foods (one to two days old) in preparing your lunch.
- Try cold leftovers, like fried chicken, burritos, or pizza.
- Try hot leftovers like soup, stew, chili, or macaroni and cheese.

Packing Tips
- Keep foods very hot or very cold, because food spoils quickly at room temperature.
- Pre-heat your thermos with hot, clean water before putting in hot foods and let it stand for two minutes.
- In hot weather, put a "freeze pack" in your bag to keep your lunch from spoiling.

Wrapping Tips
- Wrap lunch foods in waxed paper or in clean, recycled plastic food bags. If you use bags, make sure the printed side faces out.
- If you want lettuce in your sandwich, keep it from getting soggy by wrapping the lettuce separately in a damp paper towel. Add raw vegetables to the lettuce package, then at lunch time you can add crisp lettuce to your sandwich and enjoy a side order of veggies. The towel can now be used as a wipe for hands, face, or table.

A Healthy Meal

Here is a quick and easy sample lunch. It contains foods from all the food groups.

a hard-boiled egg
popcorn power pack
  (see recipe on opposite page)
vegetable sticks
a banana
and a carton of low-fat milk

Then have a long drink at the water fountain after recess.

This meal has LOTS of nutritional value. It provides servings from each of the food families and will help give you energy, make you grow, and control your body temperature. It will also help give you strong and healthy eyes, hair, skin, nerves and brain, teeth and bones, muscles, heart, blood and stomach. (See page 48 for complete details on your daily needs.)

The Well-planned Lunch

Throughout the day, your body needs a variety of foods from each of the food families. A well-planned lunch can help satisfy some of these daily needs. As you read through this book, you can choose lunch recipes and tips from any of the food families. Then all you have to do is add foods from several other families to complete your lunch. Remember to choose the LOTS foods more often than the LESS or LEAST foods as you consult the Shop Fit List on page 9.

Popcorn Power Pack

Here is a good grain choice filled with high energy nutrients.

Makes 6 two-cup servings.

Ingredients:
- 8 cups freshly popped popcorn
- 2 cups unsweetened dry cereal
- 1 cup plain toasted croutons
- 1 cup tiny unsalted pretzels
- ½ cup dry roasted peanuts
- 2 tablespoons melted margarine
- 1 teaspoon Worcestershire sauce
- ½ teaspoon each of garlic, chili, and onion powder
- ½ cup raisins (optional)

Method:
1. MIX first 5 ingredients.
2. MIX remaining ingredients (except raisins).
3. POUR over popcorn mix.
4. TOSS well, then spread evenly on a cookie sheet.
5. BAKE at 300° for 15 minutes, stirring once.
6. TURN OFF oven and let cool.
7. MIX in raisins if you like.
8. STORE in an airtight container.

Sandwiches to Go

Sandwiches are probably the most common lunch. They are a good, portable meal that can be packed with many of the nutrients your body needs. *Try some of these delicious sandwich combinations:*

Standard ingredients:
  roast beef with mustard
New toppings to try:
  radish slices
  cucumber slices
  green pepper rings

Standard ingredient:
  chicken or turkey
New toppings to try:
  cranberry sauce
  thinly sliced celery
  thinly sliced apple

Standard ingredient:
  peanut butter
New toppings to try:
  raisins
  chopped dates
  chopped prunes
  thinly sliced apple
  banana

Make a Sandwich
Experiment by making the most deliciously nutritious sandwich you can. Pick your combination from the ingredients listed inside the giant sandwich on the facing page. Have fun and be creative. Circle your choices and turn back to the Shop Fit List on page 9 to check out the nutritional value of your sandwich creation.

Banana Dog Split
Try this sample combo:
Spread peanut butter & honey (optional) on hot dog bun, wrap. Peel banana at lunch and place in bun. (Less ripe bananas are best for travelling in lunch boxes and bags.)

BREADS (GRAINS)

whole wheat	rye	pita	raisin bread	bagels	corn bread
sourdough	pumpernickel	French	rolls	tortillas	rice cakes

TOPPINGS (FRUITS & VEGETABLES)

lettuce	sprouts	green pepper	pickles	olives	diced celery	raisins	apple	crushed pineapple
tomato	cucumber	onion rings	salsa	grated carrot	radish	banana	applesauce	orange pieces

FILLINGS (PROTEINS & DAIRY FOODS)

turkey	tuna	roast beef	cheese	hummus	salmon
chicken	ham	meat loaf	egg	refried beans	peanut butter

SPREADS (May be high in Fat/Sugar)

jam	mayonnaise	taco sauce	relish	butter	low-fat cream cheese
jelly	ketchup	mustard	margarine	cheese spread	honey

The Food Families

Now that you have discovered what nutrients and foods your body needs for top performance, it's time to look at the five basic food groups in more detail to see how they work for you.

While all the food groups have nutritional value, it is important to remember that plants can supply almost every nutrient you need. If you look at the Shop Fit List on page 9, you'll see that there are more plant foods in the LOTS area than any other. They are actually the basis of all foods.

In fact, if you look at the food chains, or eating patterns, of earth's ecosystems, you will find that plants are the "producers" of the food most of the world needs. Like all other animals on the planet, we are linked to plants as "consumers." Even when we eat the meat or milk from animals, we are simply eating other consumers who have themselves eaten the energy of plants. For example, one pound of meat comes from about five pounds of "consumed" grain and soy feed.

Every time you eat any part of any plant, you are charging yourself with the get-up-and-go found in the energy that plants store as carbohydrates. Green plants cook up their own food from the sun through a process called photosynthesis. They convert the sun's energy into food by changing water and carbon dioxide gas into oxygen and carbohydrates. Some of the carbohydrates provide energy for the plant to grow. Others are stored for future energy needs. It is this stored energy that we eat when we eat plants. You also get fine-tuning vitamins and filling fiber. Proteins, minerals, and fats are found in grains and legumes (beans), as well as in the meat, fish, eggs, and dairy foods that come from the animals who eat the plants. And that in a nutshell is the story of where all our food comes from.

CARBON DIOXIDE OXYGEN

CARBOHYDRATES

MINERAL & WATER

Meet the Families

Now let's look at five food families: grains, fruits and vegetables, proteins, dairy products, and water. And then we'll take a look at relatives of these families: the Fat and Sweet Gang. You'll discover lots of fun and easy-to-make recipes with each food group that will help you plan your lunch menu.

How rich is enriched?

Grains have been ground into flour for centuries. Over time it was found that wheat flour stored better if the wheat germ was removed, and became lighter and finer if the bran was removed.

This flour was rare and more expensive, and it became associated with prosperity. However, it also represents a loss: Wheat naturally contains carbohydrates, high-quality proteins, fiber, and small amounts of 22 vitamins and minerals. White flour, however, is almost completely carbohydrate, and enriched flour has only four nutrients added back.

So, you just missed eating 18 vitamins and minerals, fiber, and some protein if you ate a slice of refined white bread!

The Grains Family

The bread you choose to house your sandwich can be a rich source of most of the nutrients you need. Wheat, for instance, contains minerals (including phosphorus, iron, potassium, and calcium), vitamins (including niacin, thiamin, riboflavin), protein, carbohydrates, fiber, and a little fat. Take a scientific look at the inside of a grain, and you can see all those rich nutrients for yourself.

If you're not exactly convinced by looking at seed innards consider the living proof of the world population: throughout the world, whole grains—mostly rice, corn, and wheat—supply more food energy and nutrients than any other food group. Amazingly, many people eat almost nothing else and are still well-nourished. In fact, together with legumes, grains form the very foundation of a fit day's food intake.

> Write down the Grain ingredients you chose for your sandwich from page 15 and their nutritional value (LOTS/LESS/LEAST) from page 9.

Cross Section of a Grain

If you take off the outer husk, or shell, of a cereal grain, you generally see three main parts: the germ, the endosperm, and the bran.

The germ is the true seed. It is packed with vitamins, minerals, and a little fat. It is right next to the endosperm, which is made up mostly of carbohydrate, which will give energy to the germ when the seed sprouts and the plant grows. These two parts are surrounded by a protective coating of bran, which contains fiber, minerals, and vitamins. Refining usually removes the bran and germ.

Tabouleh-oolie

This recipe is great for a lunch salad or as a filling for pita bread sandwich:

Makes 6 servings.

Ingredients:
- ¾ cup bulgur (cracked wheat)
- 2 medium tomatoes, chopped
- ¼ cup chopped green onions with tops
- 2 tablespoons fresh mint (or 2 teaspoons dried mint)
- 1½ tablespoons snipped parsley
- 2 tablespoons olive oil
- ¼ cup lemon juice
- ½ teaspoon salt
- ¼ teaspoon pepper
- 1 clove garlic, crushed

Method:
1. COVER bulgur with very hot water (½ inch above bulgur) for 15 minutes. Drain if necessary.
2. ADD tomatoes, green onions, and mint.
3. BLEND remaining ingredients, then POUR OVER BULGUR MIXTURE.
4. TOSS well and REFRIGERATE at least one hour.

Pasta-mania

Here's your chance to test your taste buds. Try using different varieties of pasta and cheese:

Makes 3 - 4 servings.

Ingredients:
1 cup pasta:
whole wheat,
spinach,
tomato,
elbows,
bow ties,
shells,
or your favorite
¼ cup low-fat ricotta or small-curd cottage cheese
¼ cup grated mozzarella

OR

Substitute
¼ - ½ cup "Go for a Dip" (recipe, page 38) for ricotta, cottage, or mozzarella

Method:
1. COOK then DRAIN pasta, following the directions on the back of the package. (Ask an adult for help with this.)
2. MIX IN your cheese choice.
3. SCOOP into a warmed-up thermos. If you want to eat the dip-pasta combination, chill it in the refrigerator before putting it in a thermos.

FIT TIP

Cereal to Go

Fill a container with dry cereal about 1 inch from the top. Add milk at school - and don't forget a spoon!

Give Chips the Slip with Chips in a Zip

Try low-fat foods like pretzels, bread sticks, rice cakes, low-sugar dry cereals, or popcorn (use small amount of margarine or butter-flavored substitute instead of butter), or try making your own "Chips in a Zip."

Ingredients:

corn tortillas,
 pita bread,
 or thinly sliced bagels
small amount of vegetable oil
chili powder,
 garlic powder,
 or your favorite
 seasoning

Method:

1. BRUSH tortillas, pita, or bagels very lightly with oil.
2. SPRINKLE with seasoning.
3. STACK four at a time and cut into wedges.
4. SPREAD (one layer deep) on cookie sheet.
5. BAKE in oven at 350° until crisp (about 10 minutes).

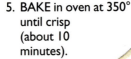

Surprise Muffins

These muffins are very low in fat. Their moistness comes from applesauce and their sweetness from honey and fruit surprises.

Makes 12 muffins.

Wet ingredients:
1½ cup unsweetened applesauce
1   egg, slightly beaten
2   tablespoons oil
¼   cup honey

Dry Ingredients:
2 cups whole wheat flour (or use 1 cup white flour, 1 cup whole wheat)
1 teaspoon baking powder
1 teaspoon baking soda
½ teaspoon cinnamon
¼ teaspoon nutmeg

Method:
1. MIX wet ingredients in a large bowl.
2. COMBINE the dry ingredients thoroughly.
3. STIR the dry ingredients into the wet ingredients until they are BARELY MIXED.
4. STIR in the surprise ingredient.
5. SPOON into a muffin tin which has been lightly greased.
6. BAKE at 375° for 20 minutes.

Surprise Ingredients:
¾ cup of ONE of the following: raisins, diced apple, grated carrots, blueberries

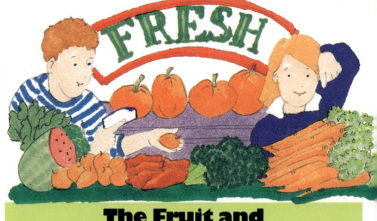

VITAMIN A
To see or not to see

When your body combines retinol (a form of vitamin A) with proteins, it forms the visual pigments of the retinal rods and cones in your eyes, which allow you to see. Your body can produce retinol from the carotene in dark yellow and dark green vegetables. The vitamin A rule of thumb is that the darker the yellow color, the more vitamin A.

Vitamin A comes in many shapes and tastes: carrot, pumpkin, sweet potato, spinach, winter squash, broccoli, apricots, cantaloupe, and turnip, mustard, and beet greens.

The Fruit and Vegetable Family

Is that sandwich you made for lunch a juicy, crunchy, high-tuned inspiration? What were your fiber and vitamin choices in the fruit and vegetable department?

Whether you picked sprouts, grated carrots, or even orange pieces, all fruits and vegetables are good choices. You really can't go wrong with fruits and vegetables. They are all filled with multiple vitamins that come in all sorts of flavors and do your body a million different favors.

For example, the vitamin C in oranges can help keep colds away, and the vitamin A in carrots can improve night vision.

Fruits and vegetables are also charged with carbohydrate energy, and their fibrous texture helps plunge your digesting food through your intestines and flush all the leftovers down the drain.

So, always remember to add fruits and vegetables to your lunch and you'll find out why people say, "An apple a day keeps the doctor away!"

VITAMIN C
To C or not to C

Vitamin C is "ascorbic" acid, from the Greek word for "no scurvy." Scurvy is a serious gum disease. Vitamin C stops scurvy and helps keep bones and teeth strong.

You can choose from many vegetables and fruits filled with vitamin C: oranges, grapefruit, lemons, tangerines, strawberries, honeydew melon, tomatoes, cauliflower, broccoli, brussels sprouts, green pepper, mustard greens, cabbage, spinach, and asparagus.

You can discover the high energy hidden in plants by eating their roots and fruits. Plants such as turnips, parsnips, radishes, carrots, beets, onions, and potatoes turn sugars into starches and store them in their roots.

Other plants store energy in the fruits of their vines or branches. The fruits of the North American squash family—acorn, banana, butternut, hubbard, and summer squashes, along with pumpkins, cucumbers, and zucchini—are loaded with high energy.

On the other hand, the five-petalled rose family, which includes apples, pears, peaches, plums, and cherries, has seeds surrounded by high-energy pulp.

One potato, two potato, three potato...salad

Potatoes are packed with nutrients, are low in fat, and provide your body with lots of carbohydrates. They produce more protein (pounds per acre) than corn, rice, wheat, or oats. Try this fiber-filled salad to get you through the day.

Makes 3 - 4 servings.

Ingredients:
3 medium potatoes
2 tablespoons chopped
    green onions
1 rib celery, chopped
¼ cup reduced-calorie
    mayonnaise
¼ cup plain low-fat yogurt
1 tablespoon mustard
    pinch of pepper

Method:
1. BOIL potatoes in water for 25 minutes, or until easily pierced by fork. Ask for an adult to help you with the boiling. (Save the vitamin-rich water to add to soups or stews.)
2. COOL, PEEL, and DICE potatoes.
3. TOSS with green onions and celery.
4. STIR IN a mixture of last 4 ingredients.
5. REFRIGERATE.

Salads to Go

Try these salad recipes. They give you lots of choice. Remember to pack them in an insulated container to keep them fresh for lunch.

Stuffed Salads

Ingredients:

Containers (choose one):
washed and hollowed out
    apple,
    green pepper,
    seeded cucumber, or
    tomato (cut from the top)
(Don't cut through the bottoms.)

Stuffing (choose one):
low-fat cottage cheese with
    a few raisins, or
tuna fish with
    diced celery, or
    chopped pickles

Method:
STUFF the container of your choice with the stuffing of your choice, and pack in an insulated container.

Fruit Salad

Makes 2-3 servings.

Ingredients:
3 favorite fruits
¼ cup orange juice

Dressing:
3 tablespoons plain, low-fat yogurt
1 teaspoon honey

Method:
1. CUT fruit into bite-sized pieces.
2. Put them in a bowl and MOISTEN with juice.
3. If you want to add dressing, drain off juice (then drink it, of course!). Mix yogurt and honey and pour over fruit.

Carrot Salad

Makes 2 servings.

Ingredients:

2 medium carrots, washed, lightly peeled, and grated

Dressing:

1 tablespoon reduced-calorie mayonnaise

1 tablespoon plain, low-fat yogurt
  orange juice

1-2 of any of these:
  raisins
  grapes
  chunks of pineapple
  pieces of cucumber
  orange sections

Method:

1. MIX mayonnaise and yogurt.
2. ADD a little juice to thin.
3. MIX together carrots and dressing plus several of the remaining ingredients.

FIT TIPS

Ready to munch

Cut-up vegetables are good to eat whenever you feel like crunching and munching. Keep some available in the refrigerator. Put them on the table before dinner and leave them afterward, then watch them disappear!

Vitamins on pancakes

Sandwich any of the following ingredients between two cold pancakes, then wrap for lunch.

- strawberries
- applesauce
- pureed fresh or canned fruits
- bananas
- experiment for yourself!

Beans Galore

Legumes are dry beans, soy beans, lentils, split peas, and peanuts.

They come from the pea family and are noted for keeping their seeds in pods. Legumes contain protein packaged with lots of fiber and little fat, which works best for our long digestive tract.

Try legumes in
- soups like chili bean soup or navy bean soup
- salads like four-bean salad (kidney, garbanzo, lima, green)
- dips like hummus from chickpeas (recipe, page 35)
- spreads like peanut butter

Take advantage of pre–packaged legumes like
- peas in pods
- peanuts

The Protein Family

Is your sandwich going to help your body grow? If you added legumes (peanut butter, refried beans), fish, poultry (chicken and turkey), meat (beef and pork), or eggs, you added a growth ingredient. But why does protein help you grow, how does it work, and what does it mean?

Protein is different from the other nutrients you've studied so far. In addition to assisting in body performance, protein helps in body building. And even though you don't need as many servings from this food group, each bite packs a powerful plus for your body.

All the ingredients of this complex nutrient work together to help you grow taller and develop stronger muscles. Nearly one-fifth of your body weight is made up of protein. Every single cell in your body has some protein—the cells of your brain, bones, heart, liver, hair, and muscles are almost all protein.

Protein is the main nutrient in this food group, but these foods are also rich in vitamins and minerals that can help with body maintenance and energy. Niacin and thiamin, for example, help digestion, improve your appetite, make your mind sharp, and help you use energy.

You can let your taste buds help you choose proteins, but keep in mind that you can run into a lot of fat in proteins. So, go for the "LOTS" protein if you can, including meats with little fat, fish, and legumes.

Write down the Protein ingredients you chose for your sandwich from page 15 and their nutritional value (LOTS/LESS/LEAST) from page 9.

Iron Power

Iron is a mineral and is an important part of what is called "hemoglobin." Hemoglobin is a protein, found in red blood cells, that carries oxygen from your lungs to cells throughout your body. It also transports carbon dioxide away from your cells to be breathed out by your lungs. It can only do this if there is enough iron in your body. Too little oxygen and too much carbon dioxide in cells can cause fatigue. Iron also helps the body to resist infections. We find iron in liver, legumes, and beef.

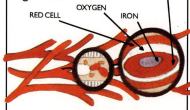

RED CELL   OXYGEN   IRON   HEMOGLOBIN

Protein ABCs

Proteins are made of amino acids. Protein from animals contains all the amino acids your body needs, so it is called COMPLETE protein. Plant proteins, on the other hand, do not have all the amino acids. They are called INCOMPLETE proteins. Even though your body can use incomplete protein, it still needs some complete protein.
Here are three ways of combining proteins to make a COMPLETE protein:

Create your own COMPLETE protein combinations, using the A, B, C guide below. Here are a couple to get you started: peanut butter on whole wheat bread, Mini-Pizza (recipe, page 44).

A+B or A+C or B+C

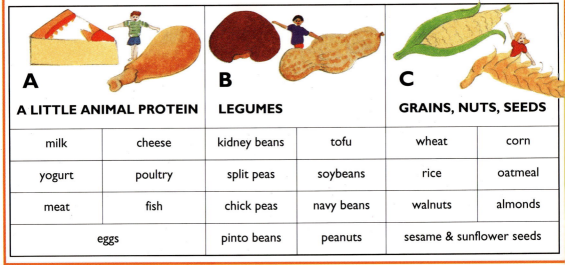

A LITTLE ANIMAL PROTEIN		LEGUMES		GRAINS, NUTS, SEEDS	
milk	cheese	kidney beans	tofu	wheat	corn
yogurt	poultry	split peas	soybeans	rice	oatmeal
meat	fish	chick peas	navy beans	walnuts	almonds
eggs		pinto beans	peanuts	sesame & sunflower seeds	

Tuna Salad Supreme

This is a great low-fat protein salad you can eat on a sandwich or pack in a container on a piece of lettuce.

Makes 2 - 3 servings.

Ingredients:
1 can tuna fish (or salmon) packed in water, drained
1 teaspoon low-fat yogurt/ mayonnaise/salad dressing
squeeze of lemon

Choose one or more:
chopped celery
apples
hard-boiled egg white
olives
grated onion
carrot
chopped pickle
cucumber
green pepper

Method:
1. MASH tuna in bowl, mixing in either yogurt, mayonnaise, or salad dressing.
2. ADD lemon juice for a tangy flavor.
3. ADD one or more of the remaining ingredients.

NOTE: *To make egg salad, substitute 2 peeled hard-boiled eggs for the tuna fish, then follow steps 1 and 2 above, adding a little salt and pepper.*

FIT TIP

Cut the Fat
Fish or light-meat poultry served without skin cuts down on extra fat. Also, broiled, roasted, and poached foods are lower in fat than sauteed or fried foods.

Hummus Dip

A great vegetable dip or spread on a bagel.

Ingredients:
2 cups canned chick peas, drained and rinsed
1 clove garlic, mashed
1-2 tablespoons peanut butter or tahini
2 teaspoons olive oil
¼ cup lemon juice
tabasco

Method:
1. PUREE chick peas in a food processor.
2. BLEND IN remaining ingredients and tabasco to your taste.

Good day, sunshine

Your body can actually make vitamin D. If you stand in the sun in your birthday suit (making sure your skin is protected with a sun screen), the oils in your skin will get turned into vitamin D by the sunlight's ultraviolet rays. There are a few problems, however, with this method of getting vitamin D. Either it gets washed away before your skin absorbs it, or not enough skin is exposed to the sun.

Fortunately, there is a simpler solution. You can also get your "D" from fortified milk, or from tasty fish like tuna, sardines, and salmon.

The Dairy Family

Did you remember your teeth and bones when you concocted your sandwich extravaganza back on page 15? Did you round it off with some phosphorus and calcium content from the dairy department? Your bones would have a really hard time standing without these minerals.

Calcium is the most plentiful mineral in your body, and about 99 percent of it is in your skeleton. (Even after your bones are done growing they are constantly being reformed.) Your bones also provide calcium for other uses in your body, like helping muscles to contract and relax, and helping your nerves deliver messages. The calcium your bones give up must be replaced by more calcium.

Obviously, your body always needs calcium. It especially needs this mineral while you are growing. Vitamin D is important here because it works with the minerals to build strong bones and teeth. Vitamin D is added to most milk.

Dairy foods also provide riboflavin, which helps in energy production, clear vision, and healthy skin. And of course dairy foods are also rich in protein. Your teeth and bones require such special attention, however, that the dairy family is grouped separately from other protein foods.

So, if you didn't add any dairy foods to your sandwich, be sure to drink a glass of milk at lunch to keep your skeleton from drooping!

Write down the Dairy ingredients you chose for your sandwich from page 15 and their nutritional value (LOTS/LESS/LEAST) from page 9.

Who's got the calcium?

Dairy foods are not the only foods with calcium. Dark-green leafy vegetables (kale, collard, mustard, and turnip greens), whole wheat and enriched bread, and broccoli are also sources of calcium. And if you want to add some crunch to your calcium, eat canned sardines and salmon—bones and all!

Go for a Dip

This low-fat dip is great to combine with your favorite dippers.
Makes 1 cup dip.

Ingredients for vegetable dippers:
bite-size pieces of fresh
  vegetables
bread sticks
pita bread
"Chips in a Zip" (recipe, page 24)

Method:
For vegetable dip, mix:
1 cup low-fat pot cheese or
   small-curd cottage cheese
1 tablespoon vinegar
½ teaspoon each of
   salt
   pepper
   dill
   dried mint
   dried parsley

Ingredients for fruit dippers:
bite-size pieces of fresh fruit

Method:
For fruit dip, mix:
1 cup low-fat pot cheese or
   small-curd cottage cheese
1-2 teaspoons of honey

NOTE: If you like a really smooth
dip, use a blender to puree the
cottage cheese.
Pack in insulated
container.

Drip-dried Yogurt

This recipe lets you make your own pot cheese, a great low-fat substitute for cream cheese or even sour cream. You can use it in the "Go for a Dip" recipe on the previous page.

Ingredients and materials:
1 pint plain, low-fat yogurt
two layers of plain white paper towels
strainer
bowl

Method:

1. LINE strainer with double layer of paper towels and SET strainer over bowl.
2. SPOON yogurt into lined strainer. Cover and PLACE in refrigerator. Leave overnight.
3. TRANSFER the yogurt into a storage container with lid.
4. SPREAD this "pot cheese" on bread, toast, crackers, or bagels.
5. STORE in refrigerator

NOTE: You have used gravity to separate the milk solids (curds) and the milk liquid (whey) in the yogurt, thus making "pot cheese."

You can use it in the "Go for a Dip" recipe on the previous page.

FIT TIP

Go for Low Fat
When selecting dairy products, it's best to choose low fat, because milk fat, and excess fat in general, can cause health problems. (See page 42 for more on fats.) Here are a few tips: Mozzarella and string cheese are good, lower-fat choices. Many markets now carry reduced-fat versions of favorite cheeses, like cheddar and Swiss. When grated cheese is needed, reduce the amount and keep the flavor by using a sharp and strong-tasting cheese.

Did you ever wonder what the percentage figures on milk mean? It is the weight of fat in the milk. Whole milk has the most fat and skim milk has no fat. Two, one, and one-half percent milks are in between.

Water Yourself

Water is actually more important to your body than food! More than half of your body is water, and it is part of every single cell. It helps carry all the other nutrients through your body, taking them to the places they have to go to do their job. It takes any leftover material out of your body. Water also helps keep your body the right temperature.

So, cool down your body and quench your thirst. Any drink will help meet your body's water needs, but you might like to know that one glass of juice can only do a part of the job that the same glass of water does.

Soft Drink Zingers

Here's a soda pop with an all-natural sweetener that will give you all the benefits of fruits and water.

Makes one 12 oz. drink.

Ingredients:
- ¼ cup 100% juice concentrate, frozen
- 4 cubes of ice
- 1 can cold seltzer water

Method:
1. Pack juice and ice in thermos. Pack can of seltzer separately.
2. At lunchtime, pour seltzer into thermos and enjoy your own fruit juice fizz. Keep adding seltzer as you drink, until it's all finished.
3. Don't forget to recycle or return your can.

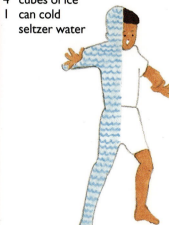

FIT TIP

If you like your water nice and cold, keep a plastic bottle in the refrigerator with your name on it. Use the kind of bottle with a straw, and you won't even have to pour it into a cup!

Make sure you rinse out your bottle every so often to keep it clean.

41

Heart Health

When it comes to eating, the wisest move for heart health and fitness is to watch out for extra fat. There are many ways fat is included in what we eat. Some fat we add to our food: mayonnaise on sandwiches, margarine on bread, sour cream on potatoes. **TIP:** Use small amounts.

Some fat we can see on foods like the edge of fat on a pork chop or the fatty skin on chicken. **TIP:** Discard the fat.

Other fats we cannot see. For example, the creamy fat in ice cream, in cookies, crackers, and hot dogs. **TIP:** Learn to read labels (see page 46) and find lower fat alternatives.

Last and definitely least, how do fats and sweets fit into your sandwich, or your lunch? If you only added a few, you made the right choice. You'll be happy to know that it's okay to eat small amounts of these tasty foods as long as you don't let them take away your appetite for fit foods. Fats and sweets are "Eat LEAST," which is not "Eat NEVER." Just remember that they only give you a spurt of energy without the other nutrients you need.

If fat is a nutrient, why aren't fat foods a food group? The fact is, fat is already in the food groups. Most dairy and protein foods — cheese, roast beef, hard-boiled eggs — naturally contain fat. Many grains, legumes, and vegetables also contain small amounts of fat. By eating servings of these foods, then, you are getting the fat your body needs to cushion your innards and keep them in place. A little fat is needed to keep you warm in the winter and cool in the summer, and to carry certain vitamins around your body.

A dab of mayonnaise or margarine in your sandwich is okay as long as you remember that a little fat goes a long way. Fat has more than twice as many calories as protein or carbohydrate. That's a lot of extra food energy for your body to store, which can be hard on your heart and blood vessels and provide more cushioning than you need. When you do eat fats, be sure to balance them with many more low-fat foods that are rich in other nutrients.

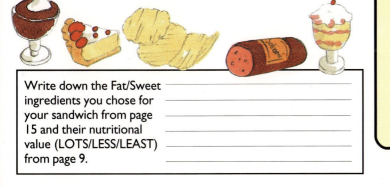

Write down the Fat/Sweet ingredients you chose for your sandwich from page 15 and their nutritional value (LOTS/LESS/LEAST) from page 9.

FIT TIP

Lower your fat choices
Watch for hidden fats in foods. Fried foods, creamy sauces, rich desserts, potato chips, and many fast foods are loaded with fat. Here are a few low-fat choices you can make, but check the Shop Fit List to avoid other fat-filled LEAST foods.

- turkey instead of bologna
- baked potato instead of fries or chips
- low-fat or non-fat dairy foods instead of regular
- frozen, low-fat yogurt instead of ice cream
- plain, vegetarian, or Mini-Pizza (recipe, page 44) instead of pizza with fatty meats or extra cheese.

Junk It Out!

Jam or jelly in your sandwich adds lots of sugar. Sugar itself isn't bad. In fact, your body turns all carbohydrates into sugar. But, as you've discovered, you need more than the sugar in carbohydrate-rich foods. Many foods that are high in simple sugar, like soft drinks, are so refined they do not have any other nutrients and are pretty useless to your body. That's why they're called "junk food," and you should eat them LEAST.

Mini-Pizza

Go into the pizza business for yourself with this recipe, and take the opportunity to control the fat you use.

Makes 4 mini-pizzas.

Ingredients:
4   medium whole wheat pitas
2   ripe tomatoes, sliced (or ½ cup tomato sauce)
1   medium zucchini (or green pepper, or mushrooms), thinly sliced
4   thin slices smoked turkey
3   ounces grated low-fat mozzarella cheese
sprinkle of dried oregano and dried basil

Method:
1. PREHEAT oven to 400°.
2. LAYER pita with ingredients.
3. BAKE for 15 minutes, or until cheese melts.
4. EAT two hot and refrigerate two to take to school.

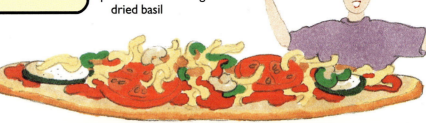

Apple Cookies

Cookies can actually be quite nutritious. Many cookie recipes can have fat reduced by ¼ or more with very little change in taste and texture. The following recipe is low in fat and includes fiber, vitamins, and minerals found in whole wheat flour, oats, apples, and raisins.

Makes 3½ dozen cookies.

Ingredients:
1   cup brown sugar
½   cup melted margarine
2   eggs
2   cups whole wheat flour
¼   teaspoon salt
½   teaspoon cinnamon
2   teaspoons baking powder
½   cup rolled oats
1½ cups shredded apple
1   cup raisins

Method:
1. PREHEAT oven to 350°.
2. MIX first three ingredients together in a bowl.
3. STIR together and ADD remaining ingredients.
4. DROP by teaspoonful onto greased cookie sheet.
5. BAKE at 350° for 12-15 minutes.
6. COOL on rack.

FIT TIP

Sweet and Healthy Choices
- a fresh, juicy apple for a snack instead of a sweetened fruit-flavored drink
- unsweetened 100 percent fruit juice for breakfast instead of a fruit drink or a soft drink
- one serving of dessert instead of two
- an *occasional* small candy bar, or share a large one with a friend instead of eating it all yourself

Shopping for Lunch

Choosing packaged foods wisely is no easy matter these days. Here are a few things to watch for when you go shopping, along with some hints to help sort things out.

Nutrition Information

Look at the serving size on the package to see if it is close to the amount you are likely to eat. Look at the calories per serving, grams of fat and percentage of calories from fat. If it is greater than 30% fat, the food is probably in the "LESS" or "LEAST" category.

Ingredients

Ingredients are always listed in order of predominance. If sugar (also known as corn sugar, dextrose, high fructose syrup, sucrose, etc.) and/or fat (lard, oil, hydrogenated oil, palm oil, etc.) is one of the first three ingredients, it is probably higher in calories and lower in nutrients. The packaged item is probably in the "LESS" or "LEAST" category.

Flashy Statements

Some products carry strong statements that imply healthy eating, when the products don't in fact offer healthy eating. For example, "reduced fat" may imply little fat when in fact the original product had so much fat that to have reduced the fat may still leave a high-fat item. "No cholesterol" does not mean "no fat." Even so, it often appears on products that never did have cholesterol in the first place and are instead high in fat!

Marketing Mystery Tour

Next time you go to the market, test your label literacy by trying to solve these marketing mysteries: Determine which brand of the following products is the best low-fat/low-junk choice. Remember to make sure the serving size is the same for the products you compare.

Note calories, grams of fat, percentage of calories from fat (if noted), and the order of ingredients.

- breakfast cereals (note carbohydrate information at bottom of label)
- cookies (watch for saturated or hydrogenated fats)
- crackers (watch for saturated or hydrogenated fats)
- canned fruit (compare juice pack, light syrup, and heavy syrup varieties)
- baked beans
- tuna (compare oil pack and water pack)
- cream cheese (compare "reduced fat" with regular)
- yogurt

What Your Body Needs Every Day

WHAT & HOW MUCH YOU NEED A DAY			SOME SAMPLE SERVINGS YOU CAN CHOOSE	
GRAINS	6 or more servings		½ bagel or bun I cup of cold cereal or popcorn	½ cup of rice, pasta, or hot cereal I roll, muffin, or slice of bread
FRUITS & VEGETABLES	5 or more servings		I piece of fruit I cup of salad greens	½ cup of vegetables or fruit ½ cup of vegetable or fruit juice
PROTEIN	2 servings		¾ cup of cooked beans I piece of fish or chicken	2 eggs 2 ounces of meat
DAIRY	3 servings		I slice of cheese I cup of yogurt	½ cup of cottage cheese I cup of milk
WATER	6 servings		4-6 ounce glass	
EXERCISE	30-60 minutes			
SLEEP	10-12 hours			

The Fitness Routine

Y ou're at the end of your lunch break and ready for recess and the rest of the day. Your stomach is quiet, but you're glad it growled at you, because you now know your body's needs inside and out. You've also become quite the smart shopper, and can put together a pretty healthy lunch.

Now take the last step to complete your fitness routine. Look at the chart on page 48 to see what you need to complete your fitness picture for today and for the future. Besides eating a healthy lunch, you need a healthy breakfast, dinner and snacks, as well as plenty of exercise and sleep.

Exercising Your Body

You need activity just as much as you need food. You also need a good night's sleep as well as a certain amount of high-energy activity.

High-energy activity does great things for your body. It can strengthen your muscles and make your body more flexible. It can relax you and even make you feel better about yourself. It also helps your appetite operate more accurately and puts the food you eat to use.

The more you move, the better your body will feel and function. It feels best if you balance your daily food energy input and exercise energy output with 30 to 60 minutes of heart-pumping, muscle-strengthening activities in addition to running around at recess. If you are not very active already, start slowly, gradually moving faster every day.

Using Your Energy

Aerobic (which means "with oxygen") exercises increase the capacity, strength, and endurance of your heart, lungs, and circulatory (blood) system. Your life depends on their health.

The best way to "aerobicise" is to do endurance-type exercises, moving your large muscle groups, like your arms and legs, together, while making your heart beat 20-26 beats per ten seconds for 20-30 minutes at a time.

Many of the activities listed in PERFORMING on the FIT STATS CHART that comes with this package will produce this healthy effect when you do them vigorously for about 30 minutes. Compare how the various activities affect your heart rate.

Flexible Pursuits

Before you begin any vigorous activity, limber up your muscles with these basic exercises. Listen to your body: grunts and groans are okay, but "Ouch!" means, "Stop."

1. Shoulder Shapers
Push shoulders up to ears, then drop shoulders towards floor. Repeat.

2. Bow Wows
Bow head to floor. Tilt head 45° to the left. Bow to floor. Tilt to the right. Repeat.

7. Reaching Torso Tilt
Holding a half-squat, stretch hands over head. Tilt at waist: reach to the right, then left. Repeat 2x.

6. Torso Tilt
Do a half-squat and hold. Put hands on head. Tilt at waist: to the left, then to the right. Repeat 2x.

5. Spin Out
Arms straight out, then move them backwards in small circles that get bigger in 8 circles.

4. Spin In
Raise arms straight up over head, then move arms forward in circles (about 8) that get smaller.

3. Fist Fingers
Put arms straight out in front of you. Make fists with your hands. Spring fingers wide open. Repeat set.

8. Gravity Pull
Cross left leg over right. Let arms slowly fall to floor, as far as possible. Repeat, then switch legs.

9. Cross, Pull, Grab
Crisscross hands behind back 8x. Pull knee to chest 2x each leg. Grab foot from behind 2x a leg.

10. Ready, Set, Go
Get in runner's "start" position. Straighten back leg. Push back heel to floor. Do 2x each leg.

11. Bear Hug
Lie on floor. Bend knees. Lift knees and grab hold. Pull into a tight hug. Breathe deeply.

12. Walk on the Ceiling
Lie on floor. Lift legs straight up. Flex feet. Walk feet back and forth 8x.

Body Building Blocks

Fit, strong muscles help you do many everyday activities, like walking, carrying things, sitting up straight, and keeping good posture. Try these exercises to strengthen specific muscle groups. Do them slowly and carefully, increasing as you feel able.

ARMS

6. Arms: Soup Can Swing
Lift your arms to shoulder height, holding soup cans for weights. Repeat 5-10x.

ARMS/CHEST

5. Arms/chest: Push-ups
Kneel on floor. Place hands (with fingers open) shoulder width apart.

Imagine you have a steel rod keeping you straight from head to knees.

Lower body of steel to floor, and back up again. Repeat 3-10x. Finish with Bear Hug.

LEGS

3. Legs: Lifting
Lie on side as shown. Lift top leg 45° up and down (don't touch the floor), first with foot extended in a point 5-10x, then flexed 5-10x.

Bend knee and rest. Roll to other side and repeat. Do two sets on each side. Repeat #2 followed by Bear Hug.

4. Legs:
In lift position, raise leg in front 45°. Hold. Flex and extend foot 5-10x. Bend knee and rest. Repeat on other side. Do 2 sets each side.

STOMACH

1. Bicycle on Your Back
Lie on floor. Place hands under small of back. Raise legs up. Bicycle fast forward downhill 20x, then uphill 20x. Repeat in reverse 20x fast and 20x slow. Do Bear Hug stretch.

2. Up and with a Twist
Lie on floor as shown. Keep small of back pressed into floor. Lift upper body 45° up and down. 5-10x.

Come up and twist to the right. Go down, then come up and twist to the left. Repeat 3-5x each side.

You and Your Body Forever

FIT TIP

Dining for Energy
Did you know that sitting down for your meals and eating slowly is more energy-efficient than eating on the run? You know better when you are satisfied and should stop eating. So, be sure to savor and enjoy the energy you eat.

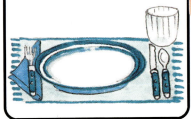

Now that you are a fit kid, you know that your body runs best with good fuel, lots of use, and proper care. Eating healthy meals and exercising will help you stay fit. Brushing you hair and teeth, washing your hands, and taking a bath are also ways of keeping your body looking and feeling great.

Your body and mind also need a chance to rest every day. Sleep lets your body slow down and use less energy. When you go to sleep tonight, think of your body as a planet spinning on its axis day after

day. While the planet rests in darkness, so will you. In the morning your body and mind will feel refreshed. Remember to care for your body by following the fitness routine you've designed for yourself. Make fitness a lifetime commitment.

Index

Recipe Index

Find out more

If you have concerns about eating disorders or health problems relating to nutrition, tell your parents. They may want to talk to your doctor or nutritionist.